The Garden Experience

Keys to Realizing Your Destined Life

By

Dexter J. Peggins Jr.

Copyright 2018 © Dexter J. Peggins Jr.

First Edition: 2016

ISBN-13: 978-0-9998955-2-8

ISBN-10: 0-9998955-2-4

Dedication

This book is dedicated to my good thing, my wife, LaSandra, and our two amazing sons. It's our time!

Acknowledgments

This work is the result of an ever-evolving process that has lasted for years. The process that I speak of is a commitment to being a lifetime learner. I have been blessed beyond measure to have had some great teachers in my life. Many of them are not teachers in the academic sense; however, they have modeled life before me in both honesty and humility, and for that, I am eternally grateful.

To my wife, LaSandra, for your prayers and constant support.

To my parents, Dexter Sr. and Della, for being my superheroes. Even though you don't wear a cape or fly in the sky, you have always been there in my time of need. Thank you!

To my spiritual mother, Evangelist Valerie Gilchrist. Thank you for the power of a push. Over the years, your words have pushed me to pursue greater.

To Apostles Carl and Donna Smalls, thank you for the love and support. God allowed us to cross paths when I wanted to give up on ministry, but you saw the potential in me and sowed a seed of hope into my life.

To Prophet Jordan Sherman, I'm thankful God allowed us to connect when he did. You are a powerful gift in the Kingdom. Keep pushing!

To my friend Dr. Tim Williams. Sir, you are such a blessing. I look forward to our coffee meetings and every time we meet, I am the better for it.

To my brothers, Dimitrius and Derrick, my extended family, and to my Army family from Korea, Kansas, and Ft. Bragg, thank you for your constant support.

To Alphonso, Jamie, Dominique, Nehemiah, Michael Perry, Yannik, and Carl II. Gentlemen, you all inspire me in your own ways. I'm excited about the future because people like you are on the job of making it better.

Aliyah, thanks for planting that seed!

Shanna, thank you for being my go-to on pretty much everything!

To my Covenant, Rhema, and Restoration families. Keep contending for the faith, and remember the fight is rigged in our favor!

TABLE OF CONTENTS

Foreword 7

Preface 12

In the Beginning 17

The 1st Principle - Identity 36

The 2nd Principle - Environmental Dynamics 44

The 3rd Principl - Boundaries 51

The 4th Principle – Employing Your Gifts 57

The 5th Principle- Nuturing the Environment 65

The 6th Principle –Recognizing Attacks 71

The 7th Principle – Change Your Atmosphere 80

New Beginning 90

About the Author 97

Foreword

Having read the first release of *The Garden Experience*, I can definitely say it is a book I wish I read when I was much younger. Dexter Peggins is a professional who is always pushing to implement ways to help people reach their desires in life. I believe *The Garden Experience* will help people achieve just that. *The Garden Experience* provides a blueprint and clear steps to help you better understand your walk in life. This book teaches you how to carefully monitor and understand your environment so you will know how to navigate life more effectively. Through his writings, Dexter provided me another perspective on how I can discover new gifts and skills based on how I am being pulled in my environment.

Dominique Bond

**Founder & CEO of Ace Ambition
Augusta, GA**

I met Dexter at my oldest granddaughters' second birthday party. His then girlfriend/now wife LaSandra, who is my goddaughter, is my youngest daughters' best friend. At that time, we had no real conversation. Sometime later, LaSandra asked if I would marry her and Dexter. After a few months of counseling, I married them. Not long after, Dexter received orders and they moved to Kentucky.

For the next seven years, I had weekly Bible studies with them over the phone and provided marriage counseling when needed. By the time they moved back to Augusta, Georgia, the two had become four, and Dexter had finished his enlistment and his residency as hospital chaplain.

Since moving back to Augusta, I have watched Dexter grow in his passion for a deeper walk with the Lord. His level of hunger has driven him to achieve many accomplishments to include the writing of this book.

He refers to me as Momma G, and I couldn't be prouder if he was my natural son.

After he wrote this book, he blessed me with a copy that I immediately read and was later asked to write the foreword of this now re-released version. To God be the glory! Great things He has done in and through the life of this man who is after the heart of God. At some point in our lives, we all ask the question, who am I and why am I here? Our lives have to mean something but what? We can't possibly go through all these mountaintop and valley experiences for no reason. Could it be there is something going on so big we just can't see it? The answer is a resounding YES!

So, how do we find our way? We find our way by connecting ourselves to a tour guide. A tour guide is someone who has taken the journey before us and can therefore lead us down the path, all while helping us avoid the potholes in the road and getting slapped in the face by branches hanging from trees on our way to purpose.

In his book, *The Garden Experience*, Dexter Peggins does just that. He begins by sharing his own struggles in life. His transparency provides not only creditability to this work but also connection to his readers. *The Garden Experience* provides its readers keys to discovering the why of their struggles in a way that is palatable, whether you are a beginner in search of truth or a mature seeker who feels the need to get back to the basics and begin again.

We were all born with greatness down on the inside waiting to be birthed. So, how do we get from labor to delivery? By protecting what we are carrying. There are seven key principles within this book that will give you the instructions you need to ensure delivery. If done correctly, the real you will emerge victorious.

One of those principles speaks about boundaries or convictions. In order to achieve anything great, there must be boundaries in place to keep what you're carrying safe and free from contamination. There must be things you do to protect and things you don't do that might hinder, delay, or abort what you are carrying. There might be things others can do but you can't because they are not carrying what you are carrying.

However, this principle will not work, nor will the others, without having the first principle firmly in place. The first principle being, "Who are you?" Without knowing who you are, how will you know the proper environment needed for optimum growth? How will you know the proper use of your gifts? How will you understand the attacks and equip yourself to win?

This book is powerful, it is life-changing, and it has the ability to move you forward into a level of greatness that eyes haven't seen nor ears heard nor entered into the heart of man what is in store for those who follow the instructions masterfully laid out within its pages.

Evangelist Valerie P. Gilchrist
Founder of Esther's Purpose
Augusta, GA

Preface

I found myself at a unique juncture when I first released *The Garden Experience* in December of 2016. *The Garden Experience* was my first published work, and as normal, with first-time things, there was an undeniable feeling of excitement and anxiety. I felt a huge sense of accomplishment; I was a published author! At the time, I was the only one in my immediate circle who could boast about possessing this title. I couldn't wait to celebrate this milestone with my family; however, life had a different set of plans.

My paternal grandfather, the patriarch of my family, died the same day my book was released. I recall my feelings of excitement and accomplishment quickly subsiding as I postured myself to mourn the passing of my grandfather. During this time, my family was extremely supportive; however, I remember reasoning within myself that this was not the time to celebrate, and truthfully, it would be several months before I regained interest in the book. In hindsight, it took too long to acknowledge it was okay to mourn and to be happy in the same instance.

My grandfather, the same man who called me Reverend and Bishop; the same man who would brag and say that his grandson was the "real deal," would be proud of my accomplishment. His attitude would be that he had lived his life, and the family had the responsibility of moving forward. In moving forward, the expectation would be that we would incorporate the lessons he instilled in us, both in word and action, and to learn from his mistakes. His desire for his children, grandchildren, and great-grandchildren was simply to be better.

As it relates to transition and the power of impact, the Bible offers the following:

"Most assuredly, I say to you, unless a grain of wheat falls into the ground and dies, it remains alone; but if it dies, it produces much grain" (John 12:24).

In this regard, I'm reminded of the contextual theme of this book: a garden. In a garden, there are a number of cyclical events that take place, all designed for the success of that garden. There is a time for planting, nurturing, and harvesting, and the garden also makes provision for death; hence, the grain of wheat that dies and so produces more grain.

I have a responsibility to honor those who have sown themselves into my life. I rejoice in knowing that through these pages, you will not only receive a number of fundamental keys to living an intentional life of purpose, but you will also get the essence of some amazing people God has used to inspire me, who have taught me how to do life well.

It is with understanding and a deep sense of humility that I embrace the significance and necessity of revisiting this assignment called *The Garden*

Experience. I began the task of writing the initial book in the summer of 2016. As I worked on my manuscript from my recliner, and on some occasions from the corner table in Starbucks, I never could have imagined the impact the book would go on to have. Churches have used it to teach their Sunday school lessons, people have told me how the revelation has helped them overcome emotional and mental barriers, and it has also been used as the foundational curriculum for a life skills training at a local prison system.

You may be asking, what is it about this book that has resonated with so many people? My short answer would be that people want to know their life has meaning. Taking it a step further, people want to connect with the reason for their existence. The issue at hand is many people have yet to discover their reason for existence and tragically, many don't know how to go about finding the answer. Hence, the basis of this book. During a season of deep frustration and depression, I was led on a journey that has indelibly changed my life and subsequently the trajectory of my family. It was on this journey that I obtained revelation concerning my existence, and as a result, I was able to embrace my purpose. Through these pages, you will be presented with practical life keys I gained while going through my process—a process I have dubbed *The Garden Experience*. If applied, these keys have the ability to help you overcome the pitfalls of life and win in difficult situations. Most importantly, this book is meant to help you connect with your identity and purpose. **Welcome to *The Garden Experience*.**

In the Beginning

Help me!

Several years ago, if you had asked me to describe myself or what my purpose on earth was, I would have looked at you with a stern look of confusion. I would have given this look not out of a misunderstanding of the question; the look would have been a sign acknowledging that I was unable to answer that question. Here I was, a man in his early-thirties who had become frustrated by the monotony of my life. There was a burning desire in my soul that served as a constant reminder I was supposed to be doing something; however, I felt disconnected from the things I was really passionate about. I was stuck, and the only question I could manage to ask was, why Dexter? Why are you here? Well, to understand my story, I will summarize it for you.

I was born in the great state of Georgia at Ft. Benning in 1979 to Dexter and Della Peggins. My parents married at the tender age of 20, and they welcomed me into this world shortly after their union. My father was a young private in the Army and my mother assumed the responsibility of a homemaker. As time passed, our family grew and my parents would later welcome my younger brothers into the world. The family was off to a great start. Even though she was young, my mother took on her home-making responsibilities seriously. You could tell she was destined for it. Long before my brothers and I came along, my mother had gained experience by raising her younger siblings. My mother is a great example, and I learned key lessons in life, like loyalty and sacrifice, from her mentorship and nurturing.

My first lesson of sacrifice came when my dad was stationed on a hardship tour in Panama. My mother moved us close to family in Ft. Wayne, Indiana, for family support. This move alone gave my dad peace of mind because we were close to family and not by ourselves. Around this time, I was in the seventh grade and my middle school class had the opportunity to go on a weekend field trip to Canada. During that time, family finances were tight and my mother told me she wouldn't be able to afford to send me on the trip. However, recognizing the benefits of this opportunity as a means of giving her son exposure to a different culture, she sacrificed her sleep and energy to work countless overtime hours and extended shifts to pay for my trip.

In describing my father, I would say he was the yang to my mother's yin. Being a son of a soldier was not a cake walk. My dad carried the military discipline into everything he did. I recall at the age of five years having to put military creases in my bed sheets, lining my shoes under the bed, and having to wake up at the right time. At that age, I honestly thought he didn't love me. I felt like I was just another soldier to him. Men in our family hardly expressed emotions or openly displayed affection. Showing emotion was generally perceived as a display of weakness, and weakness was frowned upon. The interesting observation from this was that while my dad was not given to open displays of affection, he compensated for it by using intimidation. He was such a tactician in causing havoc, I dubbed his methodology as being "strategically strict." He was always intentional and calculated in his approach to sending a message. For instance, I was your typical teenager, so my room was normally in a condition of organized chaos (messy to my liking). Nevertheless, this was a prime opportunity for him to utilize his unorthodox methods of teaching, disciplining, and instructing.

One day after coming home from school, I entered my room to find everything in total disarray. There was underwear on the ceiling fan, my drawers had been emptied and dumped on the floor, and my closet had been tossed. My room was so chaotic, I thought that our house had been broken into and my room had been ransacked. I called my mom and told her I thought we had been robbed, and she told me to do a walkthrough of the rest of the house. To my amazement, everything else was in order, and upon telling my mother that the rest of the house looked fine, she responded that my father was probably responsible for "destroying" my room. It was at this moment that I realized my dad was having a drill sergeant flashback. A common practice among drill sergeants was to empty the contents of a private's locker if their locker was found to be unsecured. Drill sergeants were known for notoriously throwing underwear and socks in various locations and giving the privates a very small window of time to clean up the mess before they experienced some extreme ramifications. Recognizing that I did not want to experience any ramifications of my own, I spent the next few hours cleaning my room. When my father got home from work, he didn't say much other than, "Hmm, I see that room is clean."

Being a military family, we were always on the move, and I quickly learned how to cope and deal with the unexpected. By the time I was 11 years old, we had lived in Georgia, Hawaii, South Carolina, Texas and Indiana. Basic coping mechanisms like making friends, individuality and adaptability were an easy thing for me, even at that age. However, I was shy and often timid, and this was an issue that followed me well into my adulthood. Before leaving for Panama in 1990, my dad said to me, "Son, you are now the man of the house." I don't know what triggered in me, but from that day on, I have always considered myself a man. In retrospect, I know I didn't have the slightest idea of what it meant to be a man, but I lived up to the image of what I believed one needed to be. My childhood evaporated at that moment. Going forward, I was a man. I had to take care of my younger siblings and never let my mother down, or so I thought. Before long, I got myself in the wrong company. By 14 years old, I was sexually active, smoking, drinking, and selling marijuana. To top it off, my grades took a plunge, and I was failing in school. Change came knocking when I lost a close friend to violence. His death served as a harsh reminder of how cruel this world could be, and it caused me to be more considerate of my own mortality.

A couple years later, by the grace of God, I staggered across my high school graduation finish line. As most young people transition into college after graduation, I knew I was ill-prepared for college, so I opted for the military. I wasn't particularly excited about the notion of being on the move, and I knew that the military life would require constant movement; nevertheless, at that time, it was my best option. So, I joined the U.S Army and oddly enough, I enjoyed it. I was getting paid while seeing the world. My first duty station was in Korea, followed by a stint in Ft. Riley, Kansas. During this time, I had become a heavy drinker, a womanizer, and a fighter. I was the consummate bachelor and lived as such. It wouldn't be until several years later that I would entertain the notion of settling down.

I was in the military during the height of the United States' military involvement in Afghanistan and Iraq. It would be during my first combat deployment that I experienced a life-defining moment. While in Iraq, on July 22, 2003, in the heart of Baghdad, word spread that Saddam Hussein's sons had been killed during a military raid. Many of the Iraqi citizens were in a celebratory mood, and they showed their excitement by firing their weapons into the air. The skies lit up as if it was the 4th of July due to the tracer bullets that were being fired. Despite being on a high state of alert, I must admit the scene was oddly beautiful. While staring at the sky, I experienced my epiphany moment. I pondered the fact that I had not lived the way I should have. My relationships were not solid. In this moment, for the first time in a long time, I thought about the condition of my life. I began to reflect on the fact that I had intentionally kept some good women at bay because of my fear of commitment. As I stared at the bullets whizzing across the sky, I made a vow to God that if He showed me the right woman, I would cease my wild behavior, settle down, and be a good husband...

Upon my return in April of 2004, my brother introduced me to a very beautiful young woman. It was love at first sight. Even though I was stationed at Ft. Bragg, North Carolina, and she lived in Augusta, Georgia, we made it work. We fell for each other hard. Prior to our courtship, I knew I would have to redeploy to Iraq in the following year. I was fearful of losing her, and all I knew was that I didn't want to be deployed without securing her as my wife. So, we got married after only 6 months of dating. What we soon realized was that marriage had its own ways of waking us up. It was not a bed of roses. Finances, family priorities, and goals in life took center stage. We were not well prepared, and the other side of "I do" had become a rude awakening. My unit was set to re-deploy to Iraq in March of 2005, and we were faced with a dilemma of figuring out our living situation.

My wife had voiced her desire about acquiring an apartment while I was deployed; however, I contended that the most economical decision would be to live with family. I wanted her to move in with my mother, and I reasoned that by doing so, we could save some money for the future when I returned. Well, that didn't go well. It's a difficult undertaking for two strong-willed adult women to come together under the same roof, especially when one makes all the rules and the other is expected to follow them. While overseas on my deployment, I heard all their frustrations, and I eventually moved my wife into her own place. Our young marriage was too fragile to withstand the constant threat of miscommunication, let alone the distance from each other. Upon my return, we both tried to make it work but the emotional upheaval had taken its toll on our young marriage. We divorced in 2006. I was devastated because I had believed this was the wife God had given me. I felt a tangible strain in my heart and even began to experience panic attacks. I analyzed my mistakes, I asked the "what if" questions and I still never came to a consensus of why we couldn't get things on track. For some time, I even blamed God for how things transpired. I said, "God, if she was the one, why did you let our marriage fail?" I fell back to my old ways of drinking heavily again. I was convinced I would be an eternal bachelor, never letting anyone get that close to my heart again.

God in his wisdom wanted me to learn the lesson in life that His will prevails against all things. I would later meet a very intelligent, beautiful, loving and caring woman. We took time to get to know one another. We introduced each other to our families, and having learned my lesson from my previous relationship, our courtship went much slower and longer. She was instrumental in helping me setup my life, budgeting, goal setting and the things we would need. We became exclusive, and with time, the blessings of our parents, and the peace of God, we married. I am honored to say that at the time of this writing, we are closing in on ten years of wedded bliss.

In 2012, I embarked on one of the hardest seasons of my life. I was transitioning from the military to pursue what I perceived to be a call to ministry. I was excited about the opportunity of continuing to serve, albeit in a vastly different capacity as a hospital chaplain. During this time of working as a hospital chaplain in Louisville, Kentucky, I was forced to deal with a number of insecurities and fears that had followed for most of my life. While working as a chaplain, I encountered people from all walks of life, dealing with a myriad of diverse mental, social, and health issues. On any given day, I could find myself at the bedside of a terminally ill patient, a grieving family member, an angry staff member, and patients who passed from life to death.

I took great pride in serving my patients, and I took it incredibly hard when I had no reply for those patients in search of answers I could not provide. It was difficult to admit but eventually, I began to experience burnout. The depth of my encounters with my patients left me feeling emotionally drained and despondent. These feelings were not solely because of the intensity of my work as a chaplain, but because

I began to recognize that a number of the agonizing questions the patients had for me were some of the same questions I had for myself. Up until this point, I had experienced success in the workforce; however, I was now beginning to confront a growing and undeniable sense of unfulfillment. My unfulfillment was rooted in the awareness that I did not know my purpose in life. This reality hit me smack in my face after a particularly difficult conversation with an 83-year-old patient. This patient shared a reality that rocked me to the core of my being. He said, "Chaplain Dexter, I'm 83 years old, and I can't tell you what I did with my life... I worked most of my life to provide for my family, but now, my wife is deceased and I hardly see my kids and their families. Besides my kids, I don't have anything to show for my life. I don't know how I'm going to be remembered and that hurts! I would have done things differently if I had known what I was supposed to do."

The sentiment of this man's pain became the emphasis of my personal prayer. "God, what I am supposed to be doing?" Little did I know that this petition would become the catalyst for an amazing journey of self-discovery, personal confrontation, and liberation.

For a period of a year, I was magnetized by three chapters in the Bible. Every time I opened the Bible, I was drawn back to reading the same scriptures over and over again. This doesn't mean I did not study any of the other sixty-six books of the Bible; however, these three chapters resonated with me unlike anything else I had read. The first three chapters of Genesis served as my training grounds in this season of frustration, and in time, my frustration turned into revelation.

It was during this time that God began to bring a new level of clarity to my life. It was as though God was saying, "Your days of walking in circles are over and you can get off on this exit." I wondered how long the exit had been there. As I reflected, the realization that it had been there all along became apparent to me. I just didn't see it. The whole time I was making circles around it. A greater revelation of my purpose came to me while giving counsel to a close friend of mine. I realized there were principles in the book of Genesis that God prescribed to mankind, and those principles formed the foundation of everything, to include the validity of our very existence.

My friend launched a business because of the counsel I'd been providing, and in noticing some personal changes in my own life, coupled with observing some of my friend's business successes, I was excited to embark on a deeper study of this fountain of truth. I've always responded well to step-by-step learning models, and I knew I was onto something when the Lord clarified the simplicity of what it meant to live a purposeful life. As I continued to learn, I continued to share with my friend, and by implementing what I was sharing, his business grew exponentially. I'm proud to announce he now has employees, maintenance vehicles, and several high-profile contracts throughout the state.

God set a plan in place for humanity before humanity was established. His plan involved the necessity of us being created in his image and likeness, and that plan gained traction with the command to go forth, be fruitful, multiply, and have dominion. But what did this principle or command really mean? First and foremost, we are gods on this earth. **Psalms 82:6** reveals the following declaration: *I say, "You are gods; you are all children of the Highest."* Knowing this truth is the first step in understanding our dominion responsibility.

In our humanity, we often downplay our significance. We use cliché statements such as, "I'm only human," and in doing so, we rarely consider the totality of who we really are. Consequently, many of us have had our identities shaped by pretentious and false narratives. We believe what society says about us as opposed to accepting the truth of what God says about us. As a consequence, God's voice is suppressed because of the tainted perception we gather from hearing cleverly laid stories that have no depth and are not rooted in the word of God. At the root of these crises of identity is our failure to realize that God speaks to us from a place of design and purpose, while we have been conditioned to only recognize the language of our societal norms. This dynamic creates a conflict within ourselves as we fight the old nature, while subsequently trying to embrace the new nature that comes with accepting God's supreme leadership. Paul declares in Romans 2 that we should not be conformed by the things of this world, but we should embrace the transformation that comes as a result of a renewed mind. It takes a renewed mind to attempt to embrace the depth of what God has to say about us. Nevertheless, to do the greater works spoken of by Christ in John 14:12, this hurdle must be overcome.

Over the course of this book, I will discuss a deliberate process of self-discovery and fulfillment I have named *The Garden Experience*. I make no assertions that this book will identify the reader's individual purpose. However, I am confident that if the reader approaches the steps in this book honestly and prayerfully, there will be a radical shift in their personhood that enables them to approach their lives with intentionality and self-awareness. Through this intentionality and awareness, the reader will begin to recognize that the makings of their purpose have been with them the whole time.

And God said, "Let us make man in our image, after our likeness: and let them have dominion over the fish of the sea, and over the birds of the heavens, and over the cattle, and over all the earth, and over every creeping thing that creepeth upon the earth." And God created man in his own image, in the image of God created he him; male and female created he them. And God blessed them: and God said unto them, "Be fruitful, and multiply, and replenish the earth, and subdue it; and have dominion over the fish of the sea, and over the birds of the heavens, and over every living thing that moveth upon the earth."

Genesis 1:26-28, ASV

The 1st Principle - Identity

Who Are You?

Identity is the first principle in the realization process of self as it relates to purpose and destiny. It is paramount. Within our world, there is no place in which the question of identity does not present itself. Whether it's a questionnaire requesting information about our race, gender, or nationality or a poll requesting our political affiliation, or the nominal distinction of being labeled a "cool kid" or a nerd, labels are everywhere. There is no escaping the expectation and need to identify with a community. At birth, the first thing a child receives is not a job or a list of responsibilities; on the contrary, at birth, a child is first given a name for the sake of identification. The basic definition of identity includes the following: who someone is; the name of a person; the qualities and beliefs; and the social and cultural values, whether by nature or nurture. One can only effectively engage their environment if they know who they are. When that happens, purpose is discovered. Remember, identity is given but purpose is revealed with time. Knowledge therefore is cognizant of origin.

God is the ultimate source of our identity. Parents can name their children and give them inherent phenotypic or genotype attributes, but your identity is embedded in your truest existence in God. Only he can give that identity.

"In the beginning, God created the heavens and the earth. The earth was barren, with no form of life; it was under a roaring ocean covered with darkness." **Genesis 1:1-2, CEV**

From this scripture, God evaluated the conditions on earth. It was null and void. Earth was a desolate place without form, function, or purpose. Earth, in its barren form, violated God's very nature and character. He quickly set out to create order. We can say in human terms he "rolled up his sleeves" and went to work by bringing the earth into alignment. His divine nature cannot deal with disorderly arrangements. He institutes the process of order by speaking faith-filled words and providing leadership directives. As a result, order was restored.

Through the declaration "let there be," God *broadcasted* a vision of that in which He had purposed within Himself to be a possibility. Subsequently, His statement *motivated* the potential that existed within the elements in which He directed His speech.

What we discover in the creation account of the heavens and the earth is a long and exemplary pattern of leadership and creativity. God was in the leadership and creation business long before He created man. Therefore, God's declaration of making man in His image and likeness was the ultimate vow of confidence; God said you can do what he had done. We are made in his image and likeness, and as a result, we have the innate power to rule, have dominion, and create. Therefore, true self-discovery is the realization that humans must develop and maintain a relationship with the creator God.

Self-awareness is only possible with the realization you are from God. For the scriptures say, *"Let Us make man in Our image, according to Our likeness..."* **(Genesis 1:26, NKJV).** It is not blasphemous to embrace the fact that you are special, peculiar and created in His image and likeness. Many people are ambiguous when it comes to this principle. They feel as though they are not qualified to feel and accept the power God has expressly bestowed upon them. But without upholding this basic fact, how can one have power or hope to impact a generation with the gifts and talents that have been freely given?

"What are mere mortals that you should think about them, human beings that you should care for them? Yet you made them only a little lower than God and crowned them with glory and honor." **Psalms 8:4-5, NLT**

I say, "You are gods; you are all children of the

Most High."

Psalms 82:6, NLT

Jesus answered them, "Is it not written in your law,

'I said, "You are gods"'?"

John 10:34, NKJV

Considering these verses, the question that begs to be answered is, "If we have been fashioned after God, why would anyone choose to live beneath their birthright?" I am convinced that many people build their lives on a foundational identity that was laid by others. Consequently, if the truth of self-identity is not reconciled, the potential fallout can be disastrous. Consider the multitude of stories about people experiencing mid-life crises. Crises are often a result of an individual discovering their purposed life has not been lived. In the wake of this realization, their inner longings for unfulfilled desires begin to surface. In what seems to be an instantaneous shift, these individuals begin to act in a manner that is contradictory to their character, and in some cases, their behavior is described as being erratic. In like manner, we operate in an unpredictable nature when we fail to live in agreement with our godly image and likeness. Identity is fundamentally the most important principle in the life of any individual. If we don't come into the knowledge of ourselves and the God who made us, abuse, neglect, and constant frustration will be the markings of our existence.

Image and identity were the first things God endowed upon humanity. Adam knew who he was before he was placed in the garden (Genesis 1:26-28), and once God put him in the garden, the garden responded to his presence (Genesis 2:5-9). When you know who you are, you will spend less time reacting to your environment and more time recognizing how your environment responds to you! With a thorough grasp of the significance of identity, we are now able to proceed in the journey of living a life of purpose, on purpose.

Something to Consider

Have you ever taken the time to consider why you believe what you believe? There are a number of factors that shape our worldviews, and often times our identity plays the largest role in the formulation of our worldviews. In this chapter, and through the entirety of this book, the subject of identity is presented from the vantage point of being the person God has called you to be. Nevertheless, allow me to state that the components of identity include DNA, environment, and personal experiences. It is necessary to highlight this point because of the external influences that weigh heavily on these areas. There are behaviors that we inherit or learn from our parents; there are diverse social constructs that exist in varying environments; and there are experiences that are unique to each individual.

In regard to the examination of our belief system, we must ask ourselves if our beliefs were given to us or if we developed those beliefs on our own. In answering this question, you have the ability to challenge beliefs you don't necessarily hold as truth. This will be an invaluable tool in your process, especially as you confront behaviors and beliefs that are contradictory to what God has said about you. When you master this principle, you will recognize your decisions are truly reflective of what you believe about yourself.

Questions for Discussion

1. **Who are you and how would you describe yourself to a total stranger?**

2. **Are your actions and decisions reflective of what you say you believe about yourself?**

The 2nd Principle - Environmental Dynamics

---

*"Then the Lord God planted a garden in Eden in the east, and there he placed the man he had made. The Lord God made all sorts of trees grow up from the ground trees that were beautiful and that produced delicious fruit. In the middle of the garden, he placed the tree of life and the tree of the knowledge of good and evil. A river flowed from the land of Eden, watering the garden and then dividing into four branches. The first branch, called the Pishon, flowed around the entire land of Havilah, where gold is found. The gold of that land is exceptionally pure; aromatic resin and onyx stone are also found there. The second branch, called the Gihon, flowed around the entire land of Cush. The third branch, called the Tigris, flowed east of the land of Asshur. The fourth branch is called the Euphrates." **Genesis 2:8-14, NKJV***

In living a destined life, a person must learn and understand their environment. An automobile doesn't drive on water, neither is a kitchen built in the bathroom. Placement, in the context of experiencing what God has for you, is not limited to a geographic location. On the contrary, placement encompasses the families in which we have been entrusted, the places we work, our circles of influence, etc. The environment you have been placed in dictates the dynamics necessary for execution of duty or responsibilities, which simply speaks to understanding the need of the environment and providing what is required in that given space.

This leads to the significance of recognizing culture. Culture must be understood and defined as, a way of thinking, behaving, or working that exists in a place or organization. Also, we can say culture could be a given society that has its own beliefs, ways of life, art, etc.

Culture is what distinguishes one environment from another. The military is a great example. I am a proud veteran of the U.S. Army, and while serving, I learned the significance of this concept. The military enforces a strict set of rules and regulations called the Code of Conduct. These rules are designed to govern the actions of service members, and they are a foundational template that distinguishes military personnel from the civilian population. For example, civilians have the benefit of exercising their freedom of speech; however, the military Code of Conduct expressly forbids service members from speaking in a manner that brings discredit upon the service. Civilians entering the military must first become indoctrinated in these customs. So, as it relates to developing a culture, one must understand that it's an act of intellectual and moral education. Creating a culture incorporates expertise in care and training, and it models excellence in taste and aesthetics.

To assimilate or develop a sense of belonging, one must avoid the desire to change an environment they have yet to understand. The significance of this statement is that it protects us from taking a judgmental stance without having any evidence to support a balanced decision. In taking the time to understand the situation, you will be better suited to know what you are supposed to do.

Like a civilian entering the military, or a new hire undergoing orientation before integration, being acquainted with the people, resources, and rules that operate within your space is vital to success. Failure to incorporate this process will be counterproductive and self-defeating. Abuse is inevitable without knowing the purpose or use of a thing. We cannot overlook or dismiss the educational process. Adam was first familiarized to his environment and then assigned by function. The garden had everything he needed for both existence and mission.

Something to Consider

There are times that we often wonder if we are in the right environment. We wonder if we are doing what we are supposed to be doing. There are times we pursue certain careers or relationships based upon our perception of what we will get out of the deal. If we're honest with ourselves, there are times when encountering difficulty and the adversity of an environment leads us to believe that we are not in the right place.

Perfect conditions aren't always the measure of whether we are in the right environment. I've discovered that one of the surest ways to determine if we are in the right environment is to examine the original motive that set us on the course for being where we are. Why did you pursue that job or that relationship? Was it solely for your personal gain or do you have something to contribute?

A question that I hear quite often is "How do we become more aware of what our environments provide?"

My answer to this question is simple: do a survey. One of the first things God did when Adam was placed in the garden was to allow Adam to survey the garden and see what came from each spot.

With that in mind, I would suggest monitoring what goes on in your life. If you do a thing consistently enough, what is the normal and expected response? As you see it, mark it! As a speaker, there are certain subjects people are more inclined to hear me speak about. I am more likely to attract a larger audience if I talk about purpose as opposed to engineering. In this regards, my environment is more likely to provide money, partnerships, and opportunities from the area of discussing purpose.

When it comes to enhancing our environments, always remember that one of the best things we can do is tend to our development. Our lives serve as the proof that the world needs us. Consider the fact that there was a lot that had to happen for us as individuals to come into the world. In this regard, we can't be opposed to the notion that we are the answer to a problem; we hold the solution to a dilemma. Our environments will give evidence that it is in need of what we have, and it's our responsibility to perfect our response to that demand.

Questions for Discussion

1. Are you aware of the environmental dynamic surrounding you? How would you describe your day-to-day activities?

2. Do you see any opportunities, challenges or assignments you feel compelled to explore? Are you pursuing those opportunities? If so, how? If not, why?

The 3rd Principle
Understand the Extent of Your Boundaries

In addition to understanding your environment, you must also acknowledge the extent or known sets of parameters or limitations.

"Then the Lord God took the man and put him in the Garden of Eden to tend and keep it. And the Lord God commanded the man, saying, 'Of every tree of the garden you may freely eat; but of the tree of the knowledge of good and evil you shall not eat, for in the day that you eat of it you shall surely die.'"

Genesis 2: 15-17, NKJV

Boundaries are recognized rules about what should not be done, or limits that define behavior. Apart from the tree of the knowledge of good and evil, Adam had free reign of everything within the garden, and he had access to everything that existed within his environment. Boundaries govern the extent of your trusted domain while restricting that which is beyond your scope of function or responsibility. Road signs, shoulders, bridges or culverts guide and provide motorists a safe zone to drive. They also provide shields from hazards and reinforcement of focus to reaching destinations safely. Therefore, boundaries are meant to protect obstructions to this fundamental philosophy. Violating the boundaries can lead to breaching the laws of the environment, and subsequently, experiencing the negative consequences thereof.

Like the concept of *learning the dynamics of your environment,* understanding your boundaries is not a principle that is limited to a geographical space. Understanding your boundaries takes into consideration physical boundaries, i.e., recognizing physical limitations that may hinder your ability to complete a task or workplace boundaries, such as knowing the scope of your responsibilities and effectively utilizing your resources. Knowing the range of the boundaries undergirds one's ability to master their domain and subsequently enjoy the benefits afforded to them. Relational boundaries exist within relationships to ensure the parties involved are healthy and benefactors of the due benevolence.

> *"Everything is permitted, but everything isn't beneficial. Everything is permitted, but everything doesn't build others up. No one should look out for their own advantage, but they should look out for each other."*
> ***1 Corinthians 10:23-24, CEB***

In this example, Paul noted that our liberty could cause others to fall. This caution encourages the preservation of relationships by avoiding activities that may compromise the integrity of the connection. The boundary is the point in which offense is inevitable, and we should be careful to ensure our liberties don't violate the extent of the limits that have been identified within our relationships.

Consequently, in the third chapter of Genesis, Adam violates the instructions set forward by God.

This violation created a rift in the fellowship that existed between God and Adam.

"Then the Lord God called to Adam and said to him, 'Where are you?' So, he said, 'I heard Your voice in the garden, and I was afraid because I was naked, and I hid myself.' And He said, 'Who told you that you were naked? Have you eaten from the tree of which I commanded you that you should not eat?'"
Genesis 3:9-11, NKJV

In eating from the tree of the knowledge of good and evil, Adam crossed a predetermined boundary set by God. In addition to compromising the trust of the relationship, the subsequent result of breaching the boundary led to Adam being removed from the environment that was entrusted to his care. In the realization of our destined lives, we have a responsibility to ensure we don't violate boundaries that have been established to keep us safe.

Something to Consider

By nature, we as humans don't like to be told that we can't do something. We don't like the notion of being restricted; therefore, the topic of boundaries and limitations doesn't rank high on the interest board. Nevertheless, consider this thought: Boundaries aren't meant to prevent you from realizing your fullest potential; they are meant to keep you on track for the fulfillment of your potential.

Limitations aren't exclusive to what you cannot do, but it in the context of this chapter, limitations speak to an intentional discipline that welcomes standards. Within the framework of this disciplined state, you acknowledge that in order to reach your goals, you cannot entertain every vice or behavior that contradicts what you are endeavoring to accomplish. We are indeed people of unlimited possibilities, but certain actions and behaviors don't lend themselves to our desired goals.

Questions for Discussion

1. What are some boundaries that exist in your life to protect your destiny?

2. Do you recognize the value of these boundaries?

3. Are there any tell-tale signs that you are in violation of your boundaries?

The 4th Principle
Employing Your Gifts

"And the LORD God said, 'It is not good that man should be alone; I will make him a helper comparable to him.' Out of the ground, the LORD God formed every beast of the field and every bird of the air and brought them to Adam to see what he would call them. And whatever Adam called each living creature, that was its name. So, Adam gave names to all cattle, to the birds of the air, and to every beast of the field. But for Adam there was not found a helper comparable to him."

Genesis 2: 18-20, NKJV

In relation to the other principles, it is my belief that the employment of your gifts is where the rubber meets the road. The previous principles dealt with the concept of discovery and learning, and in doing so, they created a foundation and context in which we are to move forward with the experiential process of destiny. The employment of your gifts is a dedicated effort towards the mastery of your skills within your assigned sphere.

The principle of employing your gifts involves the application of the work that has been committed to your charge. Through the knowledge of your responsibilities and the understanding of your resources, employing your gifts affords the opportunity to demonstrate your abilities and to handle the challenges presented within the environment. Adam understood his work and did not allow singleness to deter him from performing his assigned task. He did not look around for approval before embarking on his duties of naming animals or tending to the garden. As a matter of fact, God assumed the role of observer as Adam operated with skill and efficiency. Adam did the job so well that there was no need for God to intervene, and to this day, we recognize the animals by the names given to them by Adam. Contrast that with individuals who avoid work. They look for easy things to do without regard to their assignment. They are incapable of fulfilling a known assignment. Waiting for the right conditions will never get it done.

"When someone has been given much, much will be required in return; and when someone has been entrusted with much, even more will be required."
Luke 12:48b, NLT

Adam demonstrated his ability to efficiently and effectively accomplish his work, which showed a mastery of the first precept of God's dominion mandate: to be fruitful. In being fruitful, Adam postured himself for the next phase of dominion: to multiply.

"And the LORD God said, 'It is not good that man should be alone; I will make him a helper comparable to him.'"
Genesis 2:18, NKJV

In this declaration, God pronounces there is a predetermined helper who will come along and join the work that had been given to Adam. This scripture is often viewed in the context of a matrimonial union; however, God makes the declaration of a comparable helper in relation to the work Adam was set to embark upon, and it wasn't until later in the chapter that Adam prophesied who the woman would be to him. Nevertheless, what should be noted is that the introduction of the helper was not realized prior to the initiation of the work. God had to first ensure Adam understood the assignment. If Adam had been unsure of his work, it would have been counterproductive to introduce a woman in that environment.

Incorporating someone into work you have yet to comprehend will unquestionably create confusion, frustration, and subsequent failure. There are people who have been assigned to assist you in your life; however, when we are ignorant of what we have been given to do, abuse is certain. If people were to come prior to the comprehension of the assignment and the work was a failure, the first thought would be that the people assigned to you were out to sabotage your efforts. On the contrary, what this principle reveals is that a person cannot help you if they don't know how to help you. Many people often wait for others to show up and partner in the work before they attempt to start. Unfortunately, these people fail to consider that others will show up in response to the assignment. The people God has reserved for you and your work are waiting for the invitation from God to join you in your endeavor. As you demonstrate a measure of informed productivity, God will add unto you people who will help you to be more proficient in your assignment. It is the assignment that will stimulate what has been put in them and from this stimulation, there will be a subsequent drawing of resources, a multiplication of sorts. Think about most grassroot initiatives that started as the sole vision of an individual. The individual begins to work out what they see as a possibility and over the course of time, other likeminded individuals begin to participate. Eventually, what started out as an ideal becomes a fully-fledged movement, and this is the result of employing your gifts by way of multiplication.

Something to Consider

Is it really possible to employ your gifts? Most definitely! Simply put, employing your gifts is giving your gifts an assignment and putting them to work. Knowingly and intentionally putting your gifts to work is not only for your own benefit but for the benefit of the world. A major issue people face with respect to this point is knowing how to properly appropriate what God has given to them.

We often minimize the significance of what God has given us because we don't see the value in what we have been given. Most people devalue their gifts, not because they don't like them, but because they don't recognize what they have as being a gift. Our gifts are the things that come easy to us, but not necessarily easy to others. If you are someone who has difficulty recognizing your gifts, I would suggest asking 10 different people what they think you do well. Within their answers, you will begin to notice similarities in their responses. Take note; they are most likely highlighting your gifts.

There are some significant dangers associated with this principle. There are people who struggle with identifying who they are with relation to their gifts. You are not your gifts. Your gifts are meant to help you accomplish your purpose. Sadly, many people confuse their gifts with their identity, and in doing so, they find themselves being subjected to abuse, misunderstood, and unappreciated. This happens mainly because people are exhausting your gift without getting to know you, the individual. Consequently, people who have found themselves in this position often suppress their gifts for fear of being burnt out.

Questions for Discussion

1. Can you recognize your gifts? What are some of the gifts God has given you?

2. Can you describe how your gifts work and how you are using them?

The 5th Principle
Nurturing the Environment

"And the Lord God caused a deep sleep to fall on Adam, and he slept; and He took one of his ribs, and closed up the flesh in its place. Then the rib which the Lord God had taken from man He made into a woman, and He brought her to the man. And Adam said, 'This is now bone of my bones and flesh of my flesh; She shall be called Woman, because she was taken out of Man.' Therefore, a man shall leave his father and mother and be joined to his wife, and they shall become one flesh. And they were both naked, the man and his wife, and were not ashamed."
Genesis 2:21-25, NKJV

Consider the implications of this verse: God extracted a depth of ability and unique qualities from Adam and wrapped them in a vessel called a woman. The woman was the suitable helper God acknowledged He would bring to help Adam in the work of dominion. With both Adam and Eve on the scene, working cohesively, the environment was primed to respond to them. They had the responsibility of tending and caring for the garden, and this responsibility lends itself to the third precept of dominion: fill the earth.

This scripture reveals a truth that evades many of us. Adam and Eve were naked and unashamed—an indication of cultural transparency, freedom, and liberty. In this type of environment, it was only natural for everything under their care to thrive and flourish. There were no hidden agendas, no secrets; everything was shared in total liberty. In this attitude of freedom and transparency, Adam and Eve would nurture and bring out the best in their environment. Nurturing simply means training, upbringing, and nourishing. So, Adam and Eve lived to the fullest measure of their potential, and in being true to their identity, a culture of freedom and liberty was realized in the garden. Humanity was free before God and everything under their care had the ability to live in the same freedom.

In pursuing our destined lives, we are expected to bring out the best in not only ourselves but in everything in our purview. This is the expectation God set forth when he decreed "fill the earth." We are to engage in our assignment in such a way that it facilitates growth. The growth that was realized in the Garden of Eden was due to Adam and Eve's working relationship and union.

As stated in a previous chapter, God is relational. In making humanity in the image of God, he endowed us with the wherewithal to demonstrate his manner and character. God's fellowship with His creation was uninhibited, with nothing to hide; hence, Adam and Eve's nakedness. Trust was inevitable because there was literally nothing to hide; unfortunately, in today's world, our vulnerabilities often pose a challenge. Connecting with others can often be challenging because it requires a level of transparency. Often, we shun the notion of being vulnerable for fear of what others may think, and consequently, it is in these missed opportunities that we fail to make genuine connections and to help others in their growth.

Why didn't God just name the animals Himself? The animals came to Adam, because God placed in Adam what the animals needed. He was in charge. Many times, the people and situations that come into our lives are there by design. God often allows these occurrences to take place because we have the solution or ability to address what has been brought forward. In dealing with the matter from our truest self, we can also help others set course for their own destiny. If Adam and Eve were limited by fears of transparency, they would have been ineffective in their ability to govern.

Something to Consider

If you are anything like me, you often yearn for an assurance that you are doing what's necessary. As it relates to this chapter, one may ask, how do I know what is required from my environment? I have come to realize the environment has no issues informing you of what is needed. However, I believe our response is incumbent of a few things.

I believe we have to be sensitive to what is going on inside us. We must be aware of our internal signals when certain situations arise. What is the stimulation or compelling factor that makes us respond the way we do to given situations? Is your response consistent with the issue?

Secondly, we have to be observant to what's going on in our world and have the compassion to respond in accordance to what we know needs to be done.

From there, as we work out what we desire to do and see, our work will cause growth to take place.

Questions for Discussion

1. **In pursuing our destined lives, we are expected to bring out the best in not only ourselves but in everything in our purview.**

Are you able to recognize your opportunities to do so?

2. Describe your ideal environment. In addition to describing this environment, can you explain what you would need to do to maintain it?

The 6th Principle
Recognizing the Attacks on Purpose

_____

The serpent was the shrewdest of all the wild animals the Lord God had made. One day he asked the woman, "Did God really say you must not eat the fruit from any of the trees in the garden?" "Of course, we may eat fruit from the trees in the garden," the woman replied. "It's only the fruit from the tree in the middle of the garden that we are not allowed to eat. God said, 'You must not eat it or even touch it; if you do, you will die.'" "You won't die!" the serpent replied to the woman. "God knows that your eyes will be opened as soon as you eat it, and you will be like God, knowing both good and evil." The woman was convinced. She saw that the tree was beautiful and its fruit looked delicious, and she wanted the wisdom it would give her. So, she took some of the fruit and ate it. Then she gave some to her husband, who was with her, and he ate it, too.

Genesis 3:1-6, NLT

When Satan is first referenced in the scriptures, he introduces doubt and temptation in the garden. The temptation was not one of material gain, but the temptation came in the presentation of the knowledge of deciphering good from evil. Satan's narrative was to convince Eve that by eating the fruit of the tree of the knowledge of good and evil, it would make her like God; consequently, she lost sight of the fact that she was already like God, endowed with His attributes and characteristics.

As the story advances, Eve eats of the fruit but when she shares it with Adam, their eyes open. Their eyes were not open to some new and profound revelation; on the contrary, their eyes were opened to their own nakedness. The glory that once covered Adam and Eve had lifted, and they became keenly aware of their shortcomings rather than the potential they had once inherently enjoyed.

This passage highlights a critical component in the realization of destiny: subduing. To subdue means to conquer and bring into subjection; bring under control especially by an exertion of the will; bring (land) under cultivation; and to reduce the intensity or degree of something.

The revelation of subduing is that Adam and Eve were supposed to bring under control, reduce the intensity of, and conquer anything that attempted to come against the kingdom's culture. The attack orchestrated by Satan was simply to plant a seed of doubt. It caused Eve to second guess her identity, leading to them compromising their ability to trust in the integrity of God's word.

"She took some of the fruit and ate it. Then she gave some to her husband, who was with her, and he ate it, too." **Genesis 3:6**

Eve gave the fruit to her *husband,* which conveys that she appealed to one of Adam's functions (husband) but not the entirety of who he was as a man. Adam was more than just a husband; he was the representation of God on earth, charged with leading and expanding the garden experience. When Eve presented the fruit, her presentation appealed to the heart of her husband and not the reason of Adam.

This leads to the second point as it relates to subduing that which comes against what God has given you. Adam was "with her." This can be observed through a couple of different points of view:

1. *Adam was with Eve when Satan tempted her.* The implications of Adam being present when Eve was tempted suggest that either Adam was afraid or he did not know how to intervene in the conversation. Satan operated through the vessel of a serpent; however, both Adam and Eve had authority over every animal on the planet. The moment Adam became aware of what was spoken, he should have stepped in and rebuked the adversary. Everything Satan spoke through the serpent was in direct contradiction to the word of God, and as the steward of God's assignment, Adam had the responsibility to bring the situation under control. In times of trial, there must be a voice of reason and understanding to

challenge the thoughts that are contrary to God's directives.

2. *Adam was with Eve when she ate of the fruit.* If Adam was with Eve when she took of the fruit, this could point to Adam as the husband forgoing his responsibilities in order to please his wife. The implications of this gesture are that through the power of influence, the voice of Eve became louder and clearer to Adam than the commands of God.

3. *Adam agreed with Eve when she accepted the counsel of the adversary.* A very disconcerting possibility is that Eve told Adam what the serpent said, and he agreed with the notion that God was withholding wisdom from them.

What these possibilities ultimately point to is the fact that there was a separation that occurred between the will of humanity and the desire to fulfill the plan of God. God endowed humanity with the gift of free will, and in the truest sense of this revelation, Adam and Eve exercised their gift. In order to subdue something, there must be the decision to do so. God regularly speaks His plans and promises for His people, but to realize your purposed life, you must come into agreement with God's word. Subsequently, in coming into agreement with the plan of God, we must be mindful that temptations, distractions, and various forms of opposition will come, and we must be willing to engage and conquer the thoughts that come against our destiny.

Something to Consider

In this chapter, we spoke of the subtleness of the adversary's attack on humanity. The tactics of Satan's warfare have not changed much, if at all. In this regard, I believe that ignorance is one of the greatest attacks against purpose. What you don't know about yourself can be used against you. Satan used the enticement of information as a weapon that subsequently exposed woman's ignorance concerning her identity. This ignorance gave way to self-doubt, and self-doubt led to an unwise decision.

Ultimately, I believe the same conditions exist today, especially from an internal standpoint. We often fail to see ourselves as God does, and as a result, we fall for the tactics imposed by the adversary.

The temptations of life are unavoidable; however, we can put ourselves in positions to win when these temptations come. First, we must acknowledge there are things that have the ability to derail us from our pursuits (a temptation is a desire or enticement to do something wrong).

Secondly, while we may not be able to eliminate or control temptations, we can fight against them.

- *Avoidance* – In 1st Corinthians 10:13, we learn that temptations are common place, but God is faithful, and He will provide a way out so you can endure it. We set ourselves up for trouble when we entertain temptation.

- *Address it-* Consider the implications of giving into the temptation. What will be the end result?

We have to be able to see beyond the initial gratification of the temptation. We've all given into temptation, and I know many of our responses have been to regret giving into the temptation. We find ourselves asking, why did I do that? My question is, can we exercise that type of foresight before giving in?

Your decisions will be made from a place of being imprisoned, and as a result, you are unable to make decisions from a place of true clarity.

Questions for Discussion

1. What are some examples of attacks we experience on our purpose?

2. Have you ever been under mental attack or duress? Have you ever been manipulated, lied to, or led astray? Please describe how you responded to these events.

3. Looking back on those events, what would you have done differently?

The 7th Principle
Change Your Atmosphere

_____

*At that moment, their eyes were opened, and they
suddenly felt shame at their nakedness. So, they sewed
fig leaves together to cover themselves. When the cool
evening breezes were blowing, the man and his wife
heard the Lord God walking about in the garden. So,
they hid from the Lord God among the trees. Then the
Lord God called to the man, "Where are you?" He
replied, "I heard you walking in the garden, so I hid. I
was afraid because I was naked."* **Genesis 3:7-10, NLT**

The ability to change your environment is within
you. Humanity was placed in the garden equipped
with potential and ability, and the environment itself
was conducive and ready to respond to the
assignment God had given to humanity. As Adam
manifested the gifts that were within, he could bring
forth the best out of his environment. Whatever fell
within the sphere of Adam's influence, the
responsibility of dominion was his charge. The

responsibility of dominion belonged to Adam and Eve, and as simple as this revelation may seem, it is a truth that is often overlooked to the detriment of all who fail to grasp it.

Through their act of disobedience, Adam and Eve became aware of their nakedness, and this awareness introduced a new emotion into their world: shame. Their shame made them more conscious of their limitations rather than the potential they naturally exhibited. The severity of shame is in its ability to rob you of your future. Shame keeps you bound in remembrance of mistakes from your past.

In addition to shame, humanity became acquainted with fear. Sadly enough, Adam and Eve were fearful of the fellowship they once freely enjoyed with God.

In hearing God walk through the garden, Adam and Eve attempted to hide from God. At that moment, Adam was gripped with the question, "Where are you?" This is a question I believe God is still asking many of us. This question did not reflect that God was unaware of Adam's location, for God is omnipresent. On the contrary, Adam lost himself to himself, and God's question highlighted that Adam was acting outside of his character. Consequently, because of the disobedience in the garden, humanity has struggled to grasp the full measure of what Adam and Eve once knew as their norm.

The story of Adam and Eve's experience in the Garden of Eden ends with them being expelled from the garden.

Then the Lord God said, "Look, the human beings have become like us, knowing both good and evil. What if they reach out, take fruit from the tree of life, and eat it? Then they will live forever!" So, the Lord God banished them from the Garden of Eden, and he sent Adam out to cultivate the ground from which he had been made. After sending them out, the Lord God stationed mighty cherubim to the east of the Garden of

Eden. And he placed a flaming sword that flashed back and forth to guard the way to the tree of life.
Genesis 3:22-24, NLT

The judgment of God was decisive and forthright; nevertheless, it was not without hope. Opting to refrain from entering an expository discourse of the implications of what took place in the garden, a result of humanity's sin, is that the work which was once easy and natural became difficult.

When God created Adam, he positioned him in a place called Eden. *Strong's Concordance* defines Eden as "pleasure" (H5731), and humanity was charged with maintaining this environment. Nevertheless, when humanity violated the boundaries of their divine relationship, they were forced to relocate.

Despite humanity's departure from Eden, God never revoked humanity's dominion assignment. The scripture reveals God *"sent Adam out to cultivate the ground from which he was made"* **(Genesis 3:23).** This instruction is repetitious of the command that

God gave unto Adam when he was first placed in the garden. Dominion is the will of God, and it is the expectation that God has resoundingly placed on humanity. Secondly, as it relates to the hope of humanity, God stated that humanity had "become like us", which serves as a reaffirmation of God's design for His creation. God never changes the assignment; however, Adam's charge would be fulfilled in an environment of difficulty.

For the better part of my young adult life, I lived in a state of constant frustration. I was disappointed about a number of extenuating circumstances that had occurred in my life, and I began to feel that I was destined to live a life of unfulfilled potential. In retrospect, I understand that I was not unique in the context of living a life of frustration. I have always been familiar with people who have become resolved in their frustration, eventually settling for a life of mediocrity. During a season of intentional self-reflection and earnest prayer, God began to unravel a truth shared by the Apostle Paul.

"And we know that God causes everything to work together for the good of those who love God and are called according to his purpose for them." **Romans 8:28, NLT**

In wrestling with the implications of this scripture, God began to reveal that every test, disappointment, victory, promotion, etc. has the prospective ability to help me in my development. One of Jesus' mandates was to restore and reconcile man back unto God. I often questioned the ramifications of this restorative work, wondering what it was that I had been restored back unto. What I have discovered is that reconciliation addresses more than the renewal of my soul's condition; reconciliation reintroduces who I am in the present to the person I was always meant to be. The person I am supposed to be is a person of unlimited possibilities. In this regard, Jesus states, *"I tell you the truth, anyone who believes in me will do the same works I have done, and even greater works, because I am going to be with the Father"* **(John 14:12, NLT [emphasis added]).**

In addition to the greater works, the reconciliation brought forth by Jesus Christ reintroduced humanity to its lineage. Consider Jesus' declaration as he was challenged by those who denied his pedigree. *"Jesus replied, 'It is written in your own Scriptures that God said to certain leaders of the people, "I say, you are gods"'"* **(John 10:34, NLT).**

In regard to being reconciled to your lineage and your works, it becomes increasingly evident why the earth cries out in expectation for humanity to come into its right positioning (Romans 8:19). As I meditated on these things, God began to expound on this revelation by showing me that life in and of itself is a type of garden scenario. Just as God revealed unto Adam what existed in his garden, God longs to show us what exists in the places He puts us. From the moment I accepted this revelation, I was no longer predisposed to believing the negative things in my environment were the way they were with no hope of change. On the contrary, I now recognize that I am the change.

In this time of revelatory exploration, I discovered that as you come into the awareness of who you are, the possibilities of what God has called you to experience become more evident. God knows the potential of everything He has designated for your life: the relationships, the resources, etc. The question that begs to be answered is, how will you shape what God has committed to your trust? In this awareness, you will realize you have been surrounded by the people and resources needed to thrive in life.

When given the assignment of writing this book, I was challenged by a still small voice that said, *"Now, prove that the revelation you have been given works."* From that time forward, I have endeavored to live in the fullness and practicality of dominion. I know for certain that dominion is the life God has mandated for every person to live. In my pursuit of mastering the principles God has revealed to me, it is with much joy and excitement that I attest that these principles are indeed actually working.

Something to Consider

It is my hope that you have come to recognize that the garden in this book holds a dual meaning. In addition to being your environment, the garden is also symbolic of you, the individual, or of your subconscious mind (deep place of your heart). When you are aware of this dynamic, you become more intentional about what you allow to come within yourself (your garden).

Subsequently, when you understand and know who you are, and what's in you, you take on a command that says, I won't accept anything and everything in my space. Out of this awareness, you can begin to call forth the life you want to see as a reality.

Questions for Discussion

1. Now that *The Garden Experience* has been uniquely revealed to you, how do you plan to change your atmosphere?

2. Do you have a clearer vision of what your destined life looks like? If so, what do you see?

New Beginning

When I travel and speak with audiences about *The Garden Experience* process, they often ask me how long my journey took. I smile and tell them, "I'm still going through it." It was during a three-year process that I can say I got the hang of the principles. Nevertheless, I'm excited to admit that I am still learning new things about myself and my purpose. Through these discoveries, my capacity is being enlarged and I am being introduced to newer facets of my environment.

We can never lose sight of this most basic principle: the intent of the garden is to be fruitful. This takes on a different revelation when we elect to see ourselves as the garden. Gardens need to be tended, and this is done through processes such as cultivating, fertilizing, pruning, and the watering of plants. In this regards, you are giving attention to the things that give life to your garden to ensure its health. For example, spending quality time with your family, tending to emotional needs, prayer and meditation, taking vacations, and eliminating harmful relationships are some of the ways we tend our gardens.

A well-kept garden is enjoyable to the eyes. In addition to the visual appeal, gardens possess other inviting qualities. For instance, a flower garden can produce sweet scents that bring a sense of life to the evening and morning, hence the saying, "take time and smell the roses." The constant work in the garden bears results when neighbors, family and friends compliment the gardener, which means that people will recognize your labor. In this regard, we shouldn't be surprised when people want to spend time with us. In some cases, they may not be able to expressly say what is different about you; however, they will begin to take notice and find value in being around you.

Nevertheless, the real joy is when you start to recognize the reward for your sacrifice and to see the changes in your own self. The blossoming of flowers or the ripping of fruits brings pleasure to the owner and serves as the reward of the gardener's hard work. In this regard, you can say the gardener has reached full potential by the results seen from his or her garden. Simply put, enjoy the process of growth and take pride in the fruit yielded as a result of your maturation.

Closing Thoughts

As mentioned in the preface, I could have never imagined when I first released *The Garden Experience* the type of impact this book would have. I've received testimonies from people all over the world, and their words of affirmation and confirmation have truly inspired me. People who are well into their adulthood have told me they wished this book had been available in their teenage years because it would have saved them a lot of heartache. I have been told the book has helped people develop better relationships and also build the courage to end harmful ones. I've also been told the book has helped people gain perspective in challenging situations.

Nevertheless, despite the affirmations, there are times when my old nature wants to remind me of my insecurities and tell me I have nothing of value to offer. I was once deathly shy and uncertain of myself, and as a result, I would often shy away instead of speaking when I knew I should have. Nevertheless, I remind myself of Paul's declaration in 2 Corinthians 5:17 that I am indeed a new creation and old things have passed away. In taking ownership of this awareness, I have come to realize the areas of my greatest struggles are often the areas in which I am able to help others the most. During the formative time of my garden experience, the Lord revealed to me that He was raising me up to be a father to broken men. This was not a proclamation levied against my natural sons; on the contrary, God was revealing to me that I would be a father figure to men who needed the example of a balanced man being modeled before them. I share this story because I want to convey the truth that we aren't always privy to the process God will use to get us to our purpose.

In Jeremiah 1:12, we are given another glimpse of God's diligence in the author's assertion that God watches over his word and is careful to perform it. God follows through with what he says. I choose to accept that my frustrations and emotional hurts were necessary for the realization of my purpose. Those days of uncertainty, worry, and depression were painful, but they served as the occasion for one of the greatest gifts I could ever receive: an understanding of who I have been called to be! The lessons learned from my process paved the way for the publishing of several books and the lives of many being touched.

Just as the farmer breaks up the ground prior to the sowing of seed, I too experienced a breaking period. In my brokenness, I cried out to God for a clearer understanding of my purpose. My desire to realize my purpose led to the process of the garden. I don't know what God has or will charge you with, but I do know that on the other side of your garden experience, there is something truly amazing and most certainly needed.

If you are not operating in the fullness of your potential, make up your mind to get started now. There are things you can implement right now that will help you to grow in the capacity of your potential. Be committed to being a perpetual learner. If you are not committed to improving, you're limiting the extent of your service. Make yourself accountable. Connect with people who can push you to obtain higher heights. Connect with people who will pray for you and can call you out if you're not fully committing to the process.

When pursuing your purpose, be advised that doubt will attempt to come against you; however, you don't have to become a victim of tormenting thoughts. Celebrate your small victories. In doing this, you are able to track your progress and take confidence in knowing God is with you, encouraging you to move higher in your faith.

This world needs you, and I hope you are ready to accept the responsibility of being everything God has called you to be. I pray God blesses you beyond measure and from this day forward, you begin to live a life of purpose, on purpose!

About the Author

Dexter Peggins Jr. is the CEO and founder of Kingdom Solutions Consulting. With a practical approach to advisement and a desire to help people reach the fullness of their potential, Dexter is quickly becoming a sought-out leader in the area of life transformation. For close to 20 years, Dexter has helped countless people experience transformation in their personal, professional, and spiritual lives. Dexter's mantra is simple; "Live a life of purpose, on purpose!"

Having an innate ability to inspire, motivate, and instruct, Dexter serves as a mentor, adviser, and consultant to business and spiritual leaders going through transition, and to emerging leaders looking to make their mark in the world.

Dexter is a husband, father, business owner, author, veteran, leader, political influencer, and most importantly an ambassador of God. He holds a bachelor's degree in Christian ministry, and a master's in public administration. In addition to being a business owner, he serves on the boards of the New Leaders Council, the Georgia Prison Re-Entry Initiative, Department of Juvenile Justice, and My Brother's Keeper (Augusta, Georgia).

For more information, visit www.dexterpegginsjr.com.

Other Works by this Author

Perspective: 7 Stories from the Bible That Will Impact
Your Mindset, Life, and Leadership

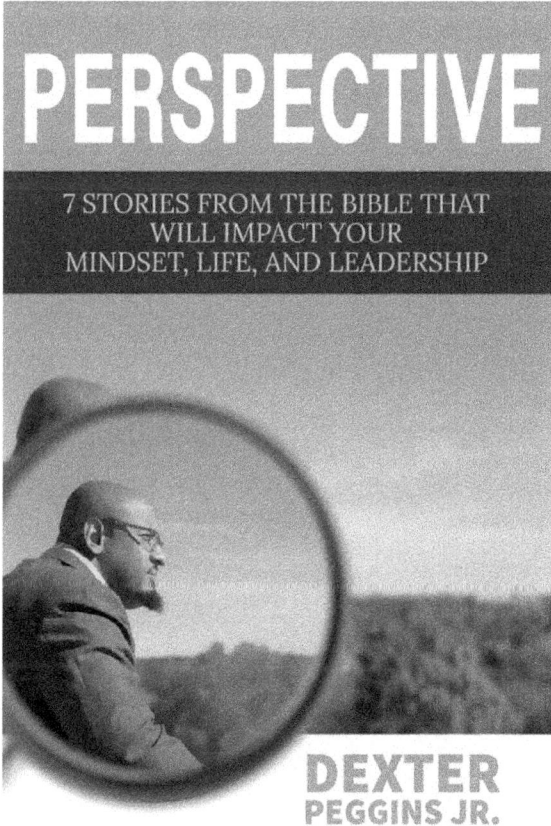

Available on Amazon

**Follow me on social media for information
concerning my new podcast coming soon!**

www.facebook.com/dexterpegginsjr/

https://www.instagram.com/kingdomsolutionsconsulting/

www.ingramcontent.com/pod-product-compliance
Lightning Source LLC
Chambersburg PA
CBHW051844040426
42447CB00006B/686